I0789298

The Story of a Special Day
Volume 306

November

1

*The 305th day of the year (306th in leap years).
There are 60 days remaining until the end of the year.*

by Michael Dobson

Timespinner
Press

Copyright © and trademarked ™ 2017 by Timespinner Press. All rights reserved, subject to the terms of licenses for photographs and other materials used herein. For a complete list of licenses and accompanying links, see the "Copyright, Credit, and Contact" section toward the end of this book. The Timespinner Press logo is a trademark of Timespinner Press.

Watch for e-book editions for Kindle, e-pub devices, and other formats from your favorite online booksellers.

For more information about the series, about us, or about your special day, please email us at editor@timespinnerpress.com.

Look for other volumes in *The Story of a Special Day,* coming often. See www.timespinnerpress.com for details and for the most recent information.

Table of Contents

For the definition of "O.S.," "CE," and "BCE" used with some dates , see the section "On Names and Dates."

Cover: "The Creation of Adam," detail from the ceiling of the Sistine Chapel by Michelangelo — the COVER STORY.

Quote of the Day

"Virtue alone is the unerring sign of a noble soul." *(La vertu, d'un cœur noble est la marque certaine.)*

Nicolas Boileau-Despréaux, French poet and critic
born November 1, 1636

Today
in
History

THER.
ACU.
MAGNA

November 1

 Michael Dobson

Labors of the Months: November, by Simon Bening

November 1 in History

While some days of the year are more famous than others, every day of the year is filled with important, exciting, and unusual events, from religious awakenings to natural disasters, from wars to breakthroughs in technology, and from tragedy to triumph.

In this section, you'll learn about all the events that make November 1 important, including the special event that makes up our cover story or event of the day. Some events you may already know about, others may be new to you, but all of them are important parts of the history of the work.

Let's explore some of the reasons why November 1 is a very special day!

A section of the Sistine Chapel ceiling

Cover Story
11/1/1512 — Sistine Chapel Ceiling Unveiled

The ceiling of the Sistine Chapel is regarded as one of the major artistic accomplishments in human civilization. It was painted between 1508 and 1512 by Michelangelo Buonarroti, one of the leading figures of the High Renaissance in Italy, and first revealed to the public on November 1, 1512.

Michelangelo was then best known as a sculptor, and had already created two of his best known works, the *Pietá* and *David*, before reaching the age of thirty. His mother died when Michelangelo was six, and he was subsequently raised by a nanny whose stonecutter husband introduced him to marble.

He attended school in Florence, at that time a major center of the arts and learning. He was an indifferent student, preferring to spend his time copying paintings. He came to the attention of the Duke de' Medici, *de facto* ruler of Florence, and under his patronage created his first noted works.

The death of his patron caused Michelangelo to leave court. During the subsequent political strife, Michelangelo left Florence and lived in several cities before he could safely return. Already known for the Pietá, he created the statue of David, arguably his most famous work, as a symbol of Florentine freedom.

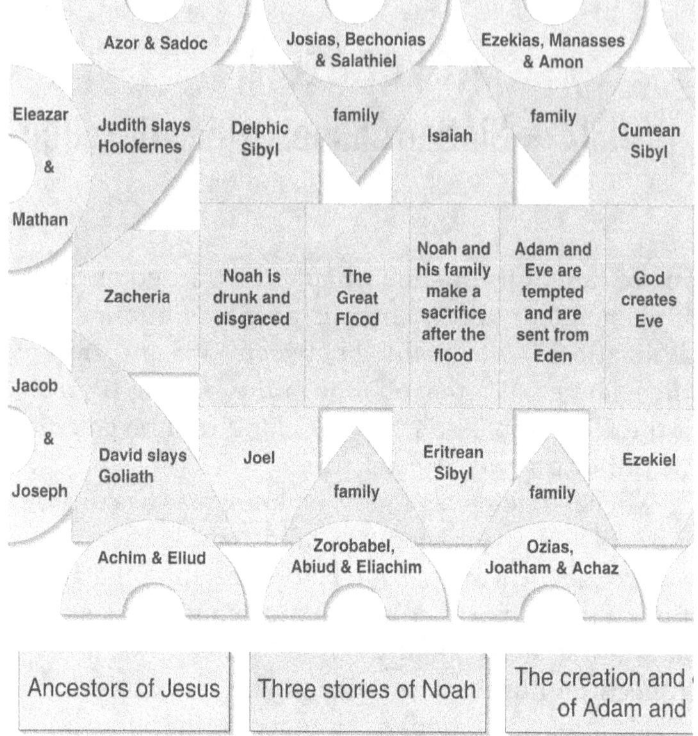

Layout of the Sistine Chapel ceiling

He was called to Rome by Pope Julius II and commissioned to build the pope's tomb. He never finished that project because he was frequently interrupted for other work — including the ceiling of the Sistine Chapel, a chapel in the Apostolic Residence of the Pope in Vatican City.

Interestingly, Michelangelo didn't want the job, as he was much less experienced as a painter than as a sculptor. There is a claim that a rival architect, who

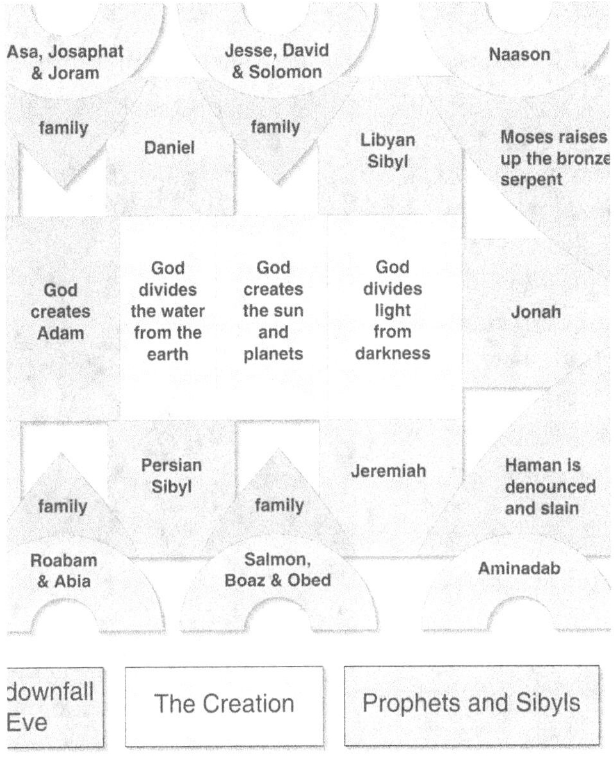

(Credit: Begoon, CC BY-SA 3.0)

resented him, persuaded the pope to choose Michelangelo for the job in hopes that he would fail.

Instead, Michelangelo designed and executed a complex masterpiece that covered over 500 square meters and contained over 300 figures. It depicted the Creation, the Fall of Man, the Promise of Salvation, and the Genealogy of Christ.

Nine episodes from the Book of Genesis form the center: God's creation of the earth, His creation of humankind and their fall from grace, and the state of humanity as represented by Noah and his family.

Many of the individual paintings that make up the ceiling are masterpieces in their own right. The philosopher and playwright Johann Wolfgang Goethe wrote, "Without having seen the Sistine Chapel, one can form no appreciable idea of what one man is capable of achieving."

Michelangelo is not the only painter represented in the Chapel. Although the ceiling and the altar painting, *The Last Judgment*, are his, a team of Reinaissance painters that included Botichelli created a series of frescoes that cover the remaining walls.

Portrait of Michelangelo, by Jacopino del Conte

The Sistine Chapel receives millions of visitors each year, and is listed as a World Heritage Site by UNESCO. It is still used as a chapel, and hosts the most important services during the Papal Calendar, unless the Pope is traveling.

What Happened on November 1?

From the creation of great works of engineering and art, to devastating wars and natural disasters, thousands of years of history have left their mark on each and every day. Here are some important events that occurred on November 1. (Items with a photo or illustration are boxed.)

1520 — Ferdinand Magellan discovers and navigates the **Strait of Magellan**, which connects the Atlantic and Pacific Oceans just south of mainland South America.

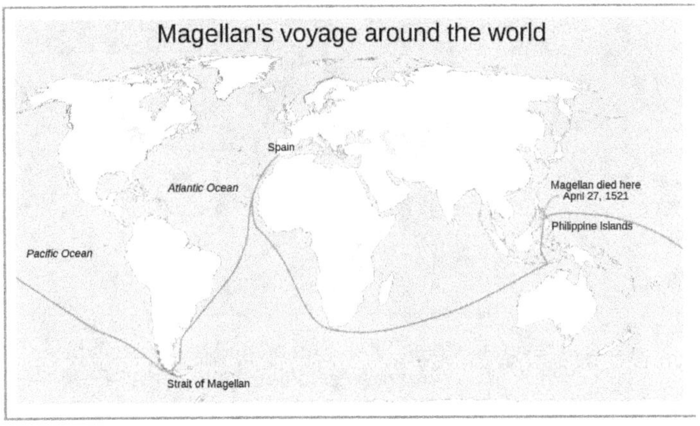

Map of Magellan's voyage (Image: Messer Woland and Petr Dlouhý, CC BY-SA 3.0)

1604/1611 — Shakespeare's *Othello* is performed for the first time at Whitehall Palace, London, on November 1, 1604. *The Tempest*, thought to be the last play Shakespeare wrote alone, premiered at the same location on November 1, 1611. British monarch James VI and I and his royal court were in attendance for both performances.

1765 — The **Stamp Tax,** imposed by the British parliament on its North American colonies, goes into effect. It led to the slogan "No taxation without representation," and was one of the causes of the American Revolution.

A British revenue stamp for use on printed materials in the American colonies

1800 — John Adams, second President of the United States, becomes the first president to live in the **White House,** then known as the "Executive Mansion."

1848 — The Boston Female Medical School, the **first medical school for women**, opens in Massachusetts.

1870 — The US Weather Bureau, later the **National Weather Service,** issues its first forecast.

1894 — Nicholas II, who will be the **last Tsar of Russia**, ascends the throne.

1894 — **Thomas Edison films sharpshooter Annie Oakley**, who goes on to fame as a member of Buffalo Bill's Wild West Show.

Annie Oakley (Photo: J. Wood)

1896 — *National Geographic* **publishes a photograph showing the bare breasts of a woman** for the first time in an American mainstream publication.

1897 — The first **Library of Congress** building opens its doors to the public.

1901 — **Sigma Phi Epsilon**, the largest US national male collegiate fraternity, is established.

1914 — The **first combat aerial bombing mission** in history takes place during the Italo-Turkish War, when Second Lieutenant Guilio Gavotti drops several small bombs on Turkish forces.

1918 — The **worst rapid transit accident in US history,** the Malbone Street Wreck in Brooklyn, takes place, killing at least 102 people.

1938 — In the horse racing "Match of the Century," **Seabiscuit defeats favorite War Admiral** in a stunning upset at Pimlico Race Course.

1950 — Puerto Rican nationalists **attempt to assassinate US President Harry Truman**.

1951 — **More than 6,000 US soldiers are exposed to atomic explosions** for training purposes in Operation Buster-Jangle in Nevada. Participation was not voluntary.

Seabiscuit

Operation Buster-Jangle

1952 — "Ivy Mike," the **first full-scale thermonuclear device, is detonated** by the US in the Enewetak Atoll.

1955 — The **Vietnam War officially begins.** It will last more than 19 years, ending with the fall of the South Vietnamese government. Estimates of Vietnamese deaths range from 100,000 to 3.8 million; US forces lost over 58,000.

1968 — The Motion Picture Association of America (MPAA) issues its **film rating system,** originally consisting of ratings G, M, R, and X. (M later became GP and then PG-13; X was replaced by NC-17.)

1973 — During the **Watergate scandal,** Leon Jaworski is appointed the **new special prosecutor,** following the firing of his predecessor Archibald Cox.

1982 — Honda becomes the **first Asian automobile company to produce cars in the United States.**

"Ivy Mike" mushroom cloud

Leon Jaworski

Quote of the Day

A man said to the universe:
"Sir I exist!"
"However," replied the universe,
"The fact has not created in me
A sense of obligation."

Stephen Crane, American poet
born November 1, 1871

Births
and
Deaths
November 1

Fernando Valenzuela, baseball hall of famer
born November 1, 1966 (Photo: Jerry Reuss, CC BY-SA 2.0)

Notable November 1 People

With the current world population at about seven billion people, on average about 19 million people also celebrate their birthdays on November 1 — and that isn't counting millions and millions who came before! No matter when you were born, you share your birthday with many special people whose accomplishments (and occasionally embarrassments) have been noted as part of history.

In this section, you'll meet fascinating people who share your birthday, or who died on this day in history. They're organized by what they're famous for, and then in reverse chronological order from most recent to earliest. Those who are shown in photographs or artwork have a box around them. We don't have photos of everyone, so please forgive us if your favorite person is missing.

Some of these people you've heard of, others will be new to you, but they all make up an important part of the reason that November 1 is a truly special day!

Stephen Crane, writer, born November 1, 1871

Who Was Born on November 1?

Art

Yuko Shimizu (清水 侑子), Japanese designer who created the iconic character *Hello Kitty.* *(1946)*

George Kenner, German artist interned as a civilian prisoner of war in World War I; known for over 100 paintings of POW camps . *(1878)*

View of a POW Camp, Isle of Man, 1918, by George Kenner

Business and Industry

Tim Cook, industrial engineer and executive who became CEO of Apple Inc. following the death of co-founder Steve Jobs. *(1960)*

Mitch Kapor, personal computer pioneer who founded Lotus and helped develop the Lotus 1-2-3 spreadsheet; co-founded and chaired the Electronic Frontier Foundation. *(1950)*

Umberto Agnelli, Italian industrialist and politician, CEO of Fiat and owner of the Juventus F. C. football (soccer) franchise; member of the Italian Football Hall of Fame. *(1934)*

Government and Law

Carlos Saavedra Lamas, Argentine politician who became the first Latin American to receive the Nobel Peace Prize. *(1878)*

Louis the Stammerer, King of France from 877 to 879. *(846)*

Music

Anthony Kiedis, lead singer and songwriter for the band Red Hot Chili Peppers; inducted with the rest of the band into the Rock and Roll Hall of Fame. *(1962)*

Louis II, King of France, by Louis-Félix Amiel

                                      Michael Dobson

Lyle Lovett, country singer-songwriter who won four Grammys; also known for his marriage to actress Julia Roberts. *(1957)*

Lyle Lovett (Photo: Anne Jacko, CC BY-SA 2.0)

Kinky Friedman, singer-songwriter and novelist known for his satirical work. *(1944)*

Salvatore Adamo, Italian singer of romantic ballads; one of the most commercially successful musicians worldwide with over 80 million albums sold. *(1943)*

Barry Sadler, former Green Beret medic in Vietnam; wrote the No. 1 pop hit "Ballad of the Green Berets." *(1940)*

Barry Sadler

Bill Anderson, country music singer-songwriter known for his long tenure on the radio and stage show *Grand Ole Opry*; reached No. 1 on the country charts seven times. *(1937)*

Sippie Wallace, singer-songwriter in blues and gospel, known as the "Texas Nightingale." Nominated for a Grammy in 1982. *(1898)*

Performing Arts

Jenny McCarthy, former Playboy Playmate of the Year and game show co-host, later co-host of the talk show *The View,* and known for her advocacy of alternatie medical treatments for autism. *(1972)*

Marcia Wallace, actress best known for her role as the receptionist Carol on the sitcom *The Bob Newhart Show,* and as the voice of elementary school teacher Edna Krabappel on *The Simpsons. (1942)*

Publicity photo from the "Carol's Wedding" episode of *The Bob Newhart Show.* From left, Larry Bondurant, **Marcia Wallace**, and Bob Newhart.

Betsy Palmer, actress known for the game show *I've Got a Secret* and for her role in the *Friday the 13th* film series. *(1904)*

Laura La Plante, silent film actress, most popular star for Universal Pictures in the 1920s. *(1904)*

Laura La Plante

Religion and Philosophy

Oliver Plunkett, Catholic archbishop and Primate of all Ireland; last victim of the Popish Plot, a fictional conspiracy used as a pretext for anti-Catholic actions. He was made a saint in 1975, the first new Irish saint in 700 years. *(1625)*

Science and Technology

Jan Davis, American astronaut who logged over 673 hours in space. *(1950)*

Astronaut Jan Davis on the aft flight deck
of the Space Shuttle *Discovery*, 1997

Robert B. Laughlin, shared the 1998 Nobel Prize in Physics for development the explanation of the fractional quantum Hall effect. *(1950)*

Sports

Fernando Valenzuela, Mexican baseball pitcher who played in Major League Baseball for 17 seasons; member of the Baseball Hall of Fame and the Mexican Baseball Hall of Fame. *(1960) (Photo page 20.)*

Gary Player, South African professional golfer and member of the World Golf Hall of Fame, one of only five golfers to win the Career Grand Slam. *(1935)*

Gary Player

Al Arbour, Canadian hockey player, coach, and member of the Hockey Hall of Fame; coached the second largest number of games in league history. *(1932)*

Maxie Rosenbloom, American boxer and former World Light Heavyweight champion known as "Slapsie Maxie" after receiving thousands of punches to the head. Later became an actor and television personality, remembered particularly for his role in Rod Serling's drama *Requiem for a Heavyweight*. *(1907) (Photo next page.)*

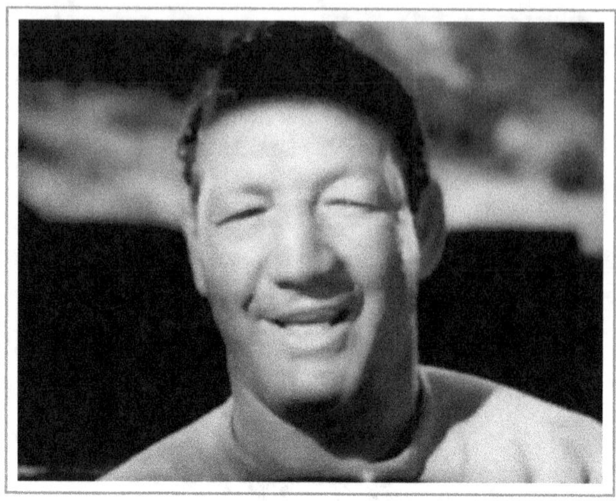

Maxie Rosenbloom in the 1941 film *Ringside Masie*

Writing and Journalism

Susanna Clarke, English author best known for her debut novel *Jonathan Strange & Mr Norrell.* *(1959)*

Larry Flynt, controversial publisher of *Hustler* and other sexually graphic materials, known for various First Amendment-related legal battles and for surviving a murder attempt. His life was chronicled in the 1996 film *The People vs. Larry Flint,* in which he was played by Woody Harrelson. *(1942)*

Edward Said, Palestinian-American author and academic known for his 1978 book *Orientalism* and for his controversial tenure on the Palestinian National Council. *(1935)*

Gordon R. Dickson, Canadian-American science fiction author best known for his "Dorsai" and "Hoka" series; member of the Science Fiction and Fantasy Hall of Fame. *(1923)*

James J. Kilpatrick, newspaper columnist and pundit known for encouraging "massive resistance" to US Supreme Court rulings outlawing racial segregation; later had a regular role as a conservative commentator on the news program *60 Minutes.* *(1920)*

Edmund Blunden, English poet, author, and critic; wrote about his World War I experiences; nominated for the Nobel Prize in Literature six times. *(1896)*

Sakutarō Hagiwara (萩原 朔太郎), Japanese poet known as the "father of modern colloquial Japanese poetry." *(1886)*

Grantland Rice, early 20th century American sportswriter known for his elegant prose. *(1880)*

Stephen Crane, American poet and novelist; his most famous work is his 1897 Civil War novel *The Red Badge of Courage. (1871) (Photo page 22.)*

Nicolas Boileau-Despréaux, French poet and critic who was influential in reforming the prevailing form of poetry. *(1636)*

Tsar Alexander III (seated, center) of Russia and family. His son and succesor Nicholas II stands directly behind him. Alexander III died November 1, 1894 (Photo: Sergey Lvovich Levitsky)

Who Died on November 1?

Government and Politics

Fred Thompson, US senator from Tennessee, radio host, and film and television actor on such programs as *Law & Order* and the movie *Die Hard 2. (2015)*

Senatorial portrait of Fred Thompson

Alexander III of Russia, tsar of Russia from 1881 until his death. Known as "the Peacemaker" because there were no major wars fought during his reign. His son, Nicholas II, was the last tsar. *(1894)*

Military and Exploration

Paul Tibbetts Jr., US Air Force general best known as the pilot who flew the B-29 Enola Gay when it dropped the atomic bomb on Hiroshima. *(2007)*

Paul Tibbetts aboard *Enola Gay* before the atomic bombing of Hiroshima (Photo: PFC Armen Shamlian)

Jean Nicolet, French-Canadian explorer who was the first European to discover and explore Lake Michigan and the first European to set foot in what is now Wisconsin. *(1642)*

Jean Nicolet arrives in Wisconsin, by Franz Edward Rohrbeck,

Music

Yma Sumac, Peruvian-American soprano famous for her five octave singing range. *(2008)*

Yma Sumac

> **Skitch Henderson,** pianist, conductor, and composer, known as the first bandleader on The Tonight Show with Johnny Carson, and as founder and conductor of the New York Pops orchestra. *(2005)*

Skitch Henderson (left) with Johnny Carson and Ed McMahon on the 1962 New Year's Eve broadcast of *The Tonight Show*

Performing Arts

Noah Beery Jr., actor best known for playing James Garner's father on the television series *The Rockford Files. (1994)*

Phil Silvers, comic actor best known for his 1950s sitcom *The Phil Silvers Show,* in which he played US Army Master Sergeant Ernie Bilko. *(1982)*

Phil Silvers as Sgt. Bilko

King Vidor, film director, producer and screenwriter whose best known films include *The Big Parade, Stella Dallas,* and *Duel in the Sun. (1982)*

James Broderick, actor known for his role as Doug on the television series *Family. (1982)*

Dixie Lee, American actress, dancer, and singer; first wife of singer Bing Crosby. *(1952)*

Dixie Lee

Religion and Spirituality

Edward Kelley, English Renaissance occultist and spirit medium who claimed to have created the legendary Philosopher's Stone that would transform base metals into gold. *(1555)*

Edward Kelley, by Thomas Pennant

Science

Theodore Hall, American Manhattan Project physicist who served as a spy for the Soviet Union, sharing information on processes for purifying plutonium and other important information. Although he was never charged because the evidence was inconclusive, he confessed publicly to his acts in 1997. *(1999)*

Severo Ochoa, Spanish physician and biochemist who shared the 1959 Nobel Prize in Physiology or Medicine for his pioneering work. *(1993)*

Sports

Walter Payton, running back for the Chicago Bears for thirteen seasons. Named to the Pro Football Hall of Fame and the College Football Hall of Fame. Mike Ditka described him as the greatest football player he had ever seen — but even greater as a human being. *(1999)*

Walter Payton

Writing and Journalism

William Styron, novelist and essayist whose best known works include *Lie Down in Darkness, The Confessions of Nat Turner,* and *Sophie's Choice. (2006)*

Ezra Pound, expatriate American modernist poet and critic. Controversially embraced Mussolini and fascism during World War II and made broadcasts criticizing the United States, for which he was detained after the war on charges of treason. During his time in custody, he wrote his masterwork, The Cantos, which was controversially awarded the Bollingen Prize by the Library of Congress in 1949. *(1972)*

Dale Carnegie, American pioneer of the self-improvement movement, famous for his 1936 best-seller *How to Win Friends and Influence People,* the basis for Dale Carnegie Training, which is still offered. *(1955)*

Alfred Jarry, French symbolist writer best known for his 1896 play *Ubu Roi. (1907)*

Theodor Mommsen, German classical scholar and archeologist who received the 1902 Nobel Prize in Literature for being "the greatest living master of the art of historical writing." *(1903)*

Quote of the Day

"We can regret what might have been...but we have no reason to be ungrateful for what there is."

Edward Said, literary theorist
born November 1, 1935

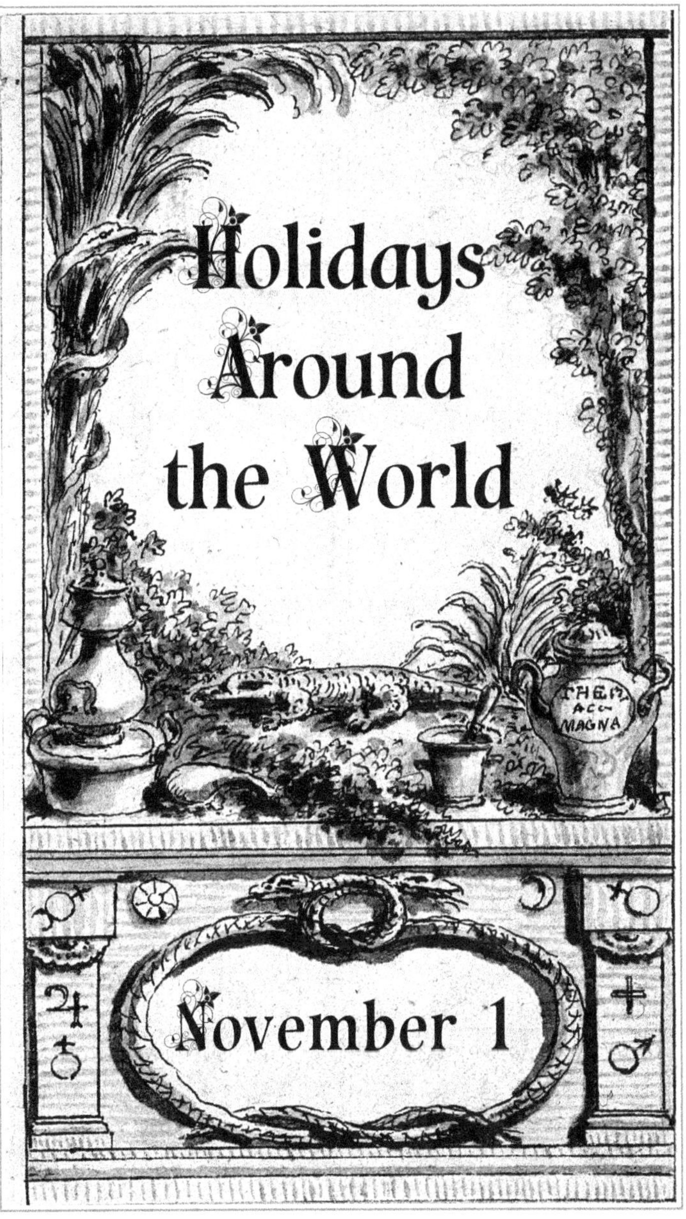

Holidays
Around
the World

November 1

Day of the Dead Musicians (Photo: Frank Kovalchek, CC BY-SA 2.0)

Holidays Around the World

If you're looking for a reason to take your special day off, you should know that every single day is a holiday somewhere in the world! Here's some of what you can celebrate on November 1!

November 1 General Events

Anniversary of the Revolution (Algeria)

The Algerian War of Independence began November 1, 1954, and ended with Algeria recognized as an independent nation on July 5, 1962. November 1 is celebrated as the Anniversary of the Revolution and July 5 as Independence Day.

Chavang Kut (Mizo)

The harvest festival of Chavang Kut is celebrated on November 1 by the Mizo people, who live in northeast India, Bangladesh, and Burma.

Coronation of King Jigme Khesar Namgyel Wangchuck, 5th Druk Gyalpo (Bhutan)

The current King of Bhutan was crowned November 1, 2008, making this day a holiday in Bhutan.

Día de Muertos (Mexico) *(photo)*

The Mexican celebration of the Day of the Dead is a public holiday involving prayer and gathering of friends and family to remember those who have died, and takes place from October 31 through November 2, in conjunction with Allhallowtide.

In addition to family remembrances, the day is marked by such treats sugar skulls, candied pumpkin, and *pan de muerto.* This celebration has been added to the Representative List of the Intangible Cultural Heritage of Humanity by UNESCO.

Independence Day (Antigua and Barbuda)

The Caribbean nation of Antigua and Barbuda became an independent state within the Commonwealth of Nations on November 1, 1981.

International Lennox-Gastaut Syndrome (LGS) Awareness Day (worldwide)

The LGS Foundation and the Epilepsy Foundation of America work to increase awareness of this childhood-onset epilepsy condition on this day.

Kannada Rajyotsava (ಕನ್ನಡ ರಾಜ್ಯೋತ್ಸವ) (Karnataka state, India)

On November 1, 1956, Kannada language-speaking regions of southern India were merged to form the state of Karnataka, celebrated as Karnataka Formation Day by Kannadigas worldwide.

Liberty Day (US Virgin Islands)

Also known as "Bull and Bread Day" or "D. Hamilton Jackson Day," this public holiday commemorates the date in 1779 that Virgin Islands labor rights leader D. Hamilton Jackson founded the first free newspaper in the Virgin Islands.

National Awakening Day (Ден на народните будители) (Bulgaria)

The nation of Bulgaria observes National Awakening Day on November 1.

National Brush Day (US)

On the day after Halloween, this day is devoted to reinforcing the importance of children's oral health by promoting good tooth-brushing habits.

English schoolchildren in the 1920s posing with toothbrushes. (Courtesy Wellcome Images, CC BY-SA 4.0)

Self-Defense Force Day (自衛隊記念日) (Japan)

On November 1, the nation of Japan honors its self-defense forces.

World Vegan Day (international)

As part of Vegan Month, November 1 is celebrated by vegans worldwide. The date was chosen to link to traditional times for feasting and celebration, such as Samhain, Halloween, and the Mexican Day of the Dead.

November 13 Food Holidays

Deep Fried Clams Day/Vinegar Day/Sundae Day (US)

In the United States, almost every day of the year is dedicated to a particular food. (Some other countries do this also, but not every day.) Sponsored by manufacturers, retailers, farmers, or simply fans, these days are often proclaimed by the President, Congress, state governors, or mayors. Given that there are more different foods than days of the year, some days honor more than one kind of food!

November 1 celebrates deep-fried clams, vinegar, and sundaes. You might put some vinegar on your deep-fried clams, but you probably don't want either of them on your sundae.

Honorary Food Months

In addition, the entire month of November is used to celebrate numerous foods. Here's a list of what to eat in the month of November!

- National Georgia Pecan Month
- National Peanut Butter Lover's Month
- National Pepper Month

- National Pomegranate Month
- National Raisin Bread Month
- Sweet Potato Awareness Month
- Vegan Month

- National Fun With Fondue Month

Cheese Fondue (for NATIONAL FUN WITH FONDUE MONTH).
(CC BY-SA 2.0)

Religious Feast Days and Holidays

All Saints' Day (most western Christian denominations)

Known variously as All Hallows' Day, Hallowmas, the Feast of All Saints, or the Solemnity of All Saints, takes place in most western Christian denominations* on November 1, the day after "All Hallows' Eve," or Halloween. The day after All Saints' Day, November 2, is All Souls' Day, commemorating those who have passed on. Together, these three days make up Allhallowtide.

Calan Gaeaf (Wales), Samhain/Beltane (various neopagan and ancient Celts)

The beginning of winter *(Samhain)* in the northern hemisphere and summer *(Beltane)* in the southern hemisphere is, along with the Welch celebration of *Calan Gaeaf,* a ceremonial event to mark the changing of the seasons. Samhain, in particular, is a pre-Christian harvest festival, elements of which survive in modern Halloween customs. These festivals normally start at sunset on October 1 and go through the following day.

---

* Eastern Orthodox denominations observe All Saints' Sunday, celebrated on the first Sunday after Pentecost. Pentecost begins seven weeks or 50 days after Easter, which means that the dates vary from year to year.

Saint Days

Each day in the year is considered a feast day for one or more saints. November 1 is the feast day of Saints Austromoine, Benignus of Dijon, Caesarius of Africa, Santa Muerte (folk Catholicism in Mexico and the southwest US).

The Eastern Orthodox tradition also venerates Saint Theolepte, Maturinus, Marcellus, Amabilis, Cledwyn, Pabiali of Wales, Dingad of Llangingat, Vigor, Gwythian, Cadfan, Caillin, Ceitho, Licinus of Angers, Floribert, Genesius of Lyon, Severinus, Germanus of Montfort, and Cosmas of Verkhoturye on November 1[†].

Moveable and Multi-Day Events

Some events take place over a specific week or time period. Start and finish dates may vary from year to year. Some events occur on different days each year (such as "fourth Saturday of a month"). These events sometimes include or take place on November 1.

Week-Long Celebrations

- Customer Service Week (US and Kenya)
- Geography Awareness Week
- National Nurse Practitioners Week
- National Split Pea Soup Week
- Mental Illness Awareness Week (US)

[†] Eastern Orthodox churches who use the Old (Julian) Calendar commemorate these saints on October 19. For an explanation of the Julian and Gregorian calendars and why dates differ, see "What Day of the Week is November 1?"

Movable Events

Moveable events that sometimes fall on November 1 include:

- Arbor Day (Samoa), first Friday
- Children's Day (South Africa), first Saturdayr
- Health Day (Turkmenistan), first Saturday
- International Stress Awareness Day (US), first Wednesday
- National Bison Day (US), first Saturday

November Honorary Months

Presidents, Congresses, and nations around the world issue proclamations recognizing particular months to honor certain causes. These events generally fall in October, though honorary months do come and go. Holidays established by states and nonprofit organizations are listed if verified.

If not otherwise specified, all months are US. There is some variation from year to year; some celebratory months get added and others get dropped. Two places to get up to date information are the current edition of *Chase's Calendar of Events* or the website Brownielocks.

Here are some honorary designations for November.

- Adopt a Turkey Month
- Aviation History Month
- Epilepsy Awareness Month
- Historic Bridge Awareness Month

- Military Family Appreciation Month
- National Adoption Month
- National Diabetes Month
- National Family Literacy Month
- National Hospice Month
- National Memoir Writing Month
- National Novel Writing Month (NaNoWriMo)
- World Sponge Month

Just for Fun

Here are a few more reasons to celebrate on the first day of November!

- Extra Mile Day
- Give Up Your "Shoulds" Day
- International Stress Awareness Day
- **National Go Cook for Your Pets Day**
- Prime Meridian Day

A parrot eating vegetables— for NATIONAL GO COOK FOR YOUR PETS DAY (Photo: Kofiwannacracker)

Quote of the Day

"November's night is dark and drear,
The dullest month of all the year."

Letitia Elizabeth Landon,
in *Traits and Trials of Early Life* (1836)

About
the
Month
of
November

November, from the *Brevarium Grimani* (c.1510)

November: The Eleventh Month

When shrieked
The bleak November winds, and smote the woods,
And the brown fields were herbless, and the shades
That met above the merry rivulet
Were spoiled, I sought, I loved them still; they seemed
Like old companions in adversity.

William Cullen Bryant, A Winter Piece

In Latin, *novem* means "nine," so it may seem strange that November is the eleventh month of the year. The original Roman calendar started in March, making November indeed the ninth month. No one is completely sure when the start of the year was moved to January, but the traditional name of November stuck.

In the northern hemisphere, November is a month in late autumn. In the southern hemisphere, November is in the springtime. May is its opposite month; spring in the north and fall in the south.

If it's not a Leap Year, November always starts on the same day of the week as February. If it is a leap year, November starts on the same day of the week as March.

November in Other Cultures

The month of November has different names in different languages. Some nations use calendars other than the Gregorian, and their months may overlap with November. In lunar-based calendars, such as the Islamic calendar, months move through the seasons. Still, many languages often have a word for November itself.

Arabic: نوفمبر (Nūfambar)

Chinese and Japanese: 十一月

Croatian: Studeni

Czech and Polish: Listopad

Finnish: Marraskuu

Greek: Νοέμβριος

Hebrew: נובמבר

Hindi: नवंबर

Old English: Blōtmōnaþ

Russian: ноябрь

November Sayings and Superstitions

Here are some sayings and superstitions associated with the month of November

- "A November bride will be liberal and kind, but sometimes cold."
- "Married in veils of November mist/Fortune your wedding ring has kissed."
- "If you wed in bleak November, only joys will come, remember."

November, by Eugène Grasset

November Symbols

Birthstone: Topaz (primarily yellow), and citrine (left). Topaz is associated with strength, tenacity, dedication and resilience. Citrine is supposed to encourage vitality and promote good health.

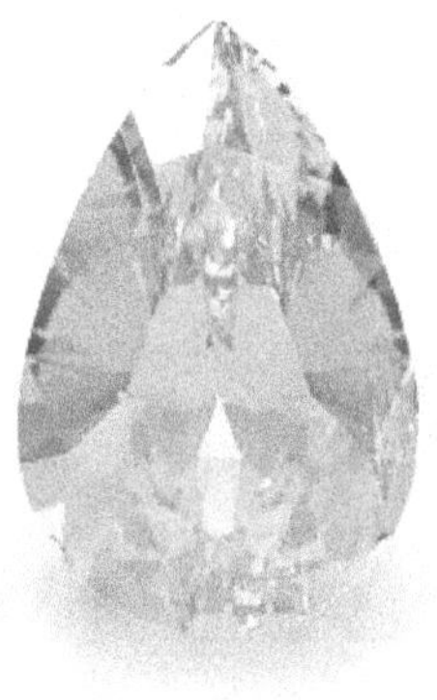

Citrine

Birth Flower: Chrysanthemum. The Chrysanthemum is associated with compassion, friendship,and joy. Red is for love, white for innocence, and yellow for unrequited love.

Chrysanthemums, by Claude Monet

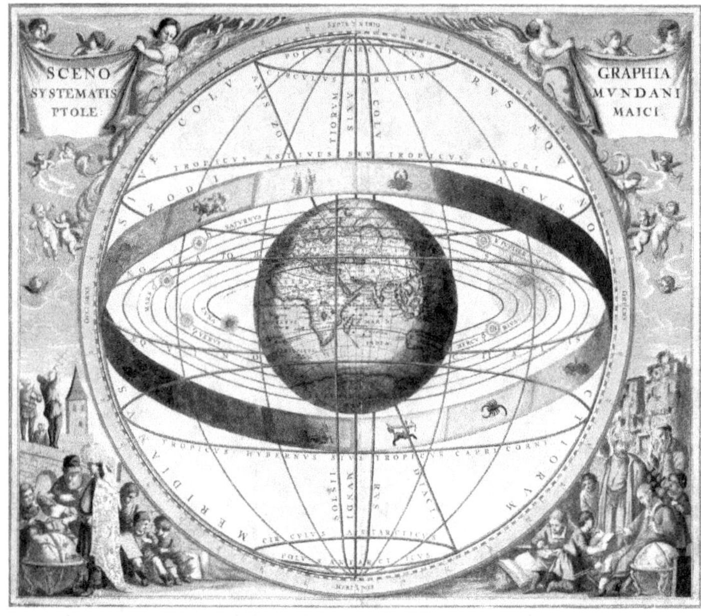

Scenography of the Ptolemaic Cosmography, by Johannes van Loon, based on Andreas Cellarius's *Harmonia Macrocosmica,* 1660

November 1 Zodiac Signs

From the perspective of someone on Earth, the Sun appears to move through the sky throughout the year, along a path astronomers call the *ecliptic plane*. The ecliptic plane is divided into twelve constellations, known as the zodiac, based on traditionally observed patterns of stars. On your birthday, you can't see your constellation, because it's in the daytime sky.

The zodiac was first developed by Babylonian astronomers about 2,500 years ago. Because they were unaware that the Earth wobbles like a spinning top (known as *precession*), they didn't make allowance for the fact that the Sun's path through the zodiac changes over time.

That means there are now two sets of dates for your birth sign. The *tropical dates* are the original Babylonian dates; the *sidereal dates* tell you where the Sun actually appears as it moves along its annual path.

For November 1, the tropical sign is **Scorpio** and the sidereal sign is **Libra**.

Libra

Tropical September 23 to October 23
Sidereal October 16 to November 15

The Babylonians considered Libra, the Scales, to be sacred to the sun god Shamash, patron of truth and justice. The Romans reassigned the scales to Astraea, the celestial virgin, better known as Virgo.

Libra is an air sign, and people born under this sign are supposed to be extroverts, socially graceful, and just. Librans are supposed to be compatible with the other air signs of Gemini and Aquarius.

Scorpio

Tropical October 23 to November 21

Sidereal November 16 to December 15

Scorpio, the Scorpion, appears in the Greek myth of the hunter Orion. Because Orion had touched the robes of the goddess Artemis, in revenge, the goddess had the scorpion kill Orion. As a reward, she placed the scorpion in the sky, where it chases Orion through the eternal night.

Scorpio is a fire sign, and people born under this sign are supposed to be determined, reserved, loyal, and secretive. Scorpios are supposed to be compatible with the water signs of Pisces and Capricorn.

Illustration by Edward Penfield

What Day of the Week is November 1?

On what day of the week does November 1 fall?

Surprisingly, this isn't an easy question. Because the calendar year is 365 days long (366 in leap years), it doesn't divide evenly by the seven days of the week.

Also, the Earth goes around the Sun in about 365-1/4 days, so a calendar tends to drift over time. That's why the same date falls on different weekdays in different years.

This is made even more complicated by a change in calendars that took place in 1582. Our modern calendar has its roots in ancient Rome, in a calendar reform conducted by Julius Caesar. Caesar commissioned mathematicians to attack the problem, and they came up with the idea of leap years, and thus standardized the calendar for centuries to come. This was called the Julian calendar.

Over time, however, the small errors in Caesar's calculation compounded. That's why Pope Gregory XIII commissioned the Gregorian calendar, used in most of the world today. Some countries converted in 1582, when the calendar was first developed; some converted later; other still haven't changed.

Gregorian and Julian aren't the only types of calendars. The Hebrew year, the Islamic year, and many other calendars are used in different parts of the world and among different people.

You can convert Gregorian dates to other calendars, including the Hebrew calendar, the Islamic calendar, and even the Mayan calendar by visiting the Fourmilab Calendar Converter at http://www.fourmilab.ch/documents/calendar/.

Chinese calendar systems are quite complex and have changed several times; a full discussion is far beyond the scope of this book. If you're interested, you can find information here: http://www.hermetic.ch/cal_stud/chinese_cal.htm.

On Names and Dates

Historians use "CE" (Common Era) and "BCE" (Before the Common Era) instead of the more common "AD" (Anno Domini, or Year of Our Lord) and "BC" (Before Christ), reflecting the fact that the year-numbering system established by the Gregorian calendar is used throughout the world in many countries not culturally Christian.

The CE/BCE designation dates back to at least 1708, and has been adopted as a standard by the United Nations and the Universal Postal Union. Because this series of books covers events and people of all nations and cultures, we use the CE/BCE terms.

The abbreviation "O.S." ("Old Style") on some dates refers to the fact that the Russian Empire did not switch from the Julian to the Gregorian calendar at the same time as the rest of Europe, and therefore some figures and events have two dates.

Also, in the Julian calendar in England in the 16th century, the year began on March 25 rather than January 1. To avoid confusion with Gregorian dates, dates between January and March were often written using both years.

People and events whose original names are not in the Western alphabet have their native names (where possible) in the appropriate script shown in parenthesis. If you are using an e-reader to access an electronic version of this book, all characters don't always display on all devices.

A 50-year brass perpetual calendar.

Quote of the Day

"Time is an illusion, lunchtime doubly so."

Douglas Adams,
from *The Hitchhiker's Guide to the Galaxy*

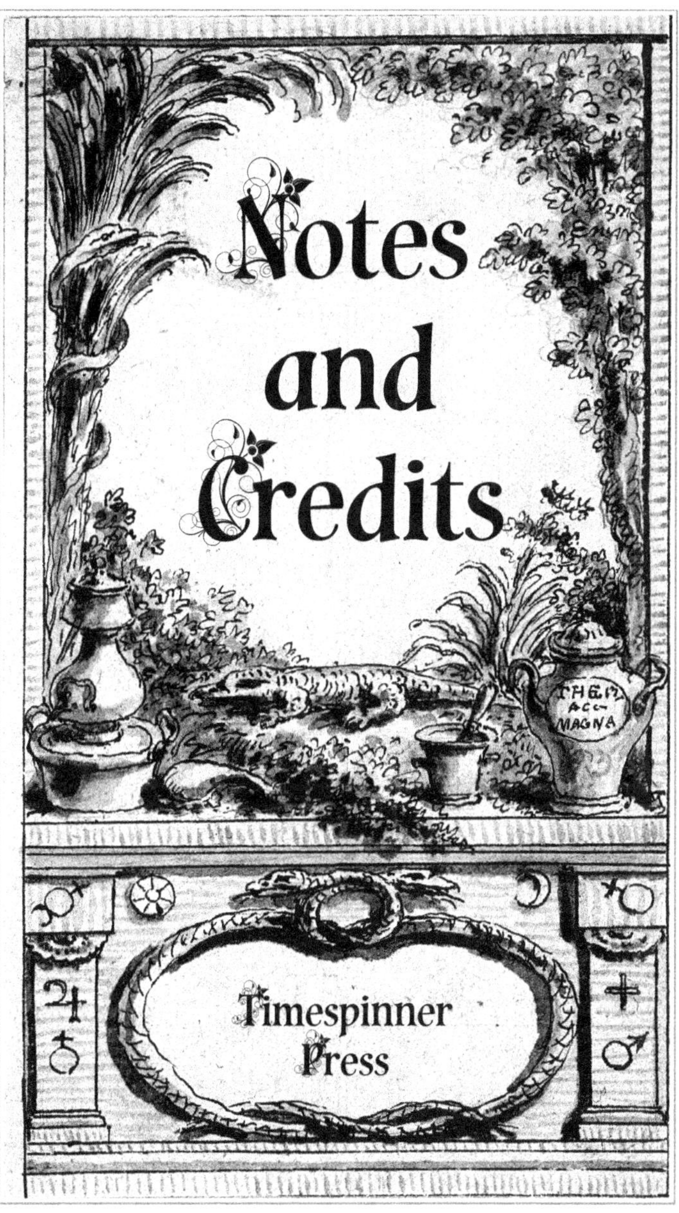

Notes and Credits
Timespinner
Press

Cartoon by John T. McCutcheon

Copyright, Credit, and Contact

Follow Us

Our blog "This Day in History" (http://
timespinnerpress.com/this-day-in-history/) features short
articles on events and people associated with each day, and
updates several times each week. Also subscribe to the
"Quote of the Day" at http://timespinnerpress.com/quote-
of-the-day/. You can get daily links by following us on
Facebook at TimespinnerPress, or on Twitter as
@sidewisethinker.

Contact Us

Find an error or a format problem? Want information about
the series, about us, or about when the volume for your
special day might be available? Please email us at
editor@timespinnerpress.com. (We also take requests if your
special day isn't yet complete. Please give us at least six
weeks' notice if possible.)

Sources

We owe a great debt to Wikipedia, which is our first stop for
research. We attempt to make independent confirmation of
all important dates and facts through a variety of other
sources.

Other sources we frequently use include the Library of
Congress; "on this day" listings from *Encyclopedia Britannica,*
the *New York Times,* and the BBC; Omniglot for the names of
months in other languages; *Chase's Calendar of Events;* and, of
course, the always essential Google.

All art and photographs are either in the public domain, used under a Creative Commons license, or with a "fair use" justification, and most frequently come from Wikimedia Commons and the Library of Congress Prints and Photographs Division.

Attribution is provided where possible, or as requested by the copyright owner, or when there is particular historical significance, listed below. For information about any particular illustration or photograph, please contact us.

Credits

1. The cover photograph of the Creation of Adam from the Sistine Chapel ceiling painted by Michelangelo circa 1511 is in the public domain because its copyright has expired.

2. The illustration of the month of November used on the back cover is from the French Gothic illuminated manuscript *Les Très Riches Heures du duc de Berry* by the Limbourg Brothers, Jean Colombe, and an intermediate painter whose name is lost to history. It is in the public domain because its copyright has expired.

3. The box graphic used on the first page is from a 1916 pamphlet entitled "Divorce versus Democracy" authored by G. K. Chesterton, originally published in London by the Society of St. Peter and St. Paul. It is in the public domain in the US because it was published prior to 1923, and is in the public domain in all countries (including the country of origin) in which the copyright time is the author's life plus 70 years or less.

4. The graphic design for the section pages in this book is from a design originally created for a pharmacy label. It is courtesy of Wellcome Images (ICV No 11073, photo V0010813), and is used here under CC BY-SA 4.0.

5. The painting "November" from *Labors of the Month* by Simon Bening, was originally published in the first half of the 16th century, and is in the public domain because its copyright has expired.

6. The photograph of the ceiling of the Sistine Chapel was taken in 2008 by Patrick Landy. It is used here under CC BY-SA 3.0.

7. The diagram of the Sistine Chapel ceiling is by "Begoon," based on works by T. Taylor and others. It is used here under CC BY-SA 3.0.

8. The portrait of Michelangelo Buonarroti by Jacopino del Conte was created circa 1535, and is in the public domain because its copyright has expired.

9. The 2006 map of Magellan's voyage was created by Messer Woland and Petr Dlouhý, based on a work by "Knutux." It is used here under CC BY-SA 3.0.

10. The photograph of Annie Oakley by J. Wood is in the public domain because its copyright has expired.

11. The 1940 photograph of Seabiscuit is in the public domain because it was first published in the US between 1923 and 1977 without a copyright notice.

12. The photograph from Operation Buster-Jangle is in the public domain as a work created by an employee of the US government as part of that person's official duties. It is from the collection of the National Nuclear Security Administration, id XX-77.

13. The photographof the Ivy Mike mushroom cloud is in the public domain as a work created by an employee of the US government as part of that person's official duties. It is from the collection of the National Nuclear Security Administraiton, id IVY-52-05.

14. The photograph of Leon Jaworski was released into the public domain by its author, University of Houston Libraries.

15. The 1991 photograph of Fernando Valenzuela was taken by Jerry Reuss, and is used here under CC BY-SA 2.0.

16. The 1895 photograph of Stephen Crane is in the public domain because its copyright has expired.

17. The 1918 painting by George Kenner, *View of a POW Camp, Isle of Man,* is photograph Art.IWM ART 17053 in the collection of the Imperial War Museums. It is in the public domain because its copyright has expired.

18. The 1837 painting *Louis II, King of France*, by Louis-Félix Amiel, is from the collection of the Palace of Versailles. It is in the public domain because its copyright has expired.

19. The 2016 photograph of Lyle Lovett was taken by Anne Jacko. It is used here under CC BY-SA 2.0.

20. The 1966 publicity photograph of Barry Sadler appeared in an advertisement in *Billboard*, January 29, 1966, issue. It is in the public domain because it was first published in the US between 1923 and 1977 without a copyright notice.

21. The 1975 publicity photograph from *The Bob Newhart Show* is in the public domain because it was first published in the US between 1923 and 1977 without a copyright notice. Traditionally, publicity photographs are not copyrighted because of the way they are intended to be used.

22. The 1924 publicity photo of Laura La Plante originally appeared in *Photoplay* magazine. It is in the public domain because it was published in the US between 1923 and 1953, and although there may or may not have been a copyright notice, the copyright was not renewed.

23. The 1967 photograph of Jan Davis is in the public domain because it is a work solely created by NASA.

24. The 2008 photograph of Gary Player was released into the public domain by its author, "Lady 11390."

25. The 1941 trailer screenshot from *Ringside Masie* is in the public domain because it was first published in the US between 1923 and 1977 without a copyright notice. Traditionally, film trailers are not copyrighted because of the way they are intended to be used.

26. The 1888 photograph of Alexander III and family by Sergey Lvovich Levitsky is in the public domain because its copyright has expired.

27. The official Senatorial photograph of Fred Thompson is in the public domain as a work created by an employee of the US government as part of that person's official duties.

28. The 1945 photograph of Paul Tibbetts and *Enola Gay* was taken by PFC Armen Shamlian, and is in the collection of the US National Archives, NWDNS-208-LU-13H-5. It is in the public domain as a work created by an employee of the US government as part of that person's official duties.

29. The painting of Jean Nicolet arriving in Green Bay, Wisconsin, in 1634 was painted in 1919 by Franz Edward Rohrbeck, and is in the public domain because its copyright has expired.

30. The photograph of Yma Sumac first appeared in the March 28, 1954, issue of *Radiocorriere*, N. 13, year XXXI. It is in the public domain in Italy, its country of origin and first publication, because its term of copyright has expired.

31. The 1962 publicity photograph from *The Tonight Show* is in the public domain because it was first published in the US between 1923 and 1977 without a copyright notice. Traditionally, publicity photographs are not copyrighted because of the way they are intended to be used.

32. The publicity photograph of Phil Silvers is in the public domain because it was first published in the US between 1923 and 1977 without a copyright notice. Traditionally, publicity photographs are not copyrighted because of the way they are intended to be used.

33. The photograph of Dixie Lee appeared in the August 1935 issue *Picture Play* magazine, published by Street & Smith. It is in the public domain because it was published in the US between 1923 and 1953, and although there may or may not have been a copyright notice, the copyright was not renewed.

34. The Thomas Pennant illustration of Edward Kelley was created prior to 1798, and is in the public domain because its copyright has expired.

35. The 1984 photograph of Walter Payton is in the public domain because it was published in the United States between 1978 and March 1, 1989 without a copyright notice, and its copyright was not subsequently registered with the U.S. Copyright Office within 5 years.

36. The photograph of a piece of art at the Musical Instrument Museum, Phoenix, Arizona, was taken by Frank Kovalchek and is used here under CC BY-SA 2.0.

37. The 1920s photograph of English children brushing their teeth is from Wellcome Images, V0030839. It is used here under CC BY-SA 4.0.

38. The 2009 photograph of cheese fondue is by "The Junes" and modified by "Zitronenpresse."It is used here under CC BY-SA 2.0.

39. The 2010 photograph of a Fledgeling Lesser Jardines Parrot eating vegetables was released into the public domain by its creator, "Kofiwannacracker."

40. The photograph of dominoes is by "Gaz," and is used here under CC BY-SA 3.0.

41. The painting "November" is from the *Brevarium Grimani*, circa 1510, and is in the public domain because its copyright has expired.

42. The 1896 postcard "November" by Eugène Grasset is in the public domain because its copyright has expired.

43. The photograph of a citrine is by Les Facettes and is used here under CC BY-SA 3.0.

44. The 1882 painting of chrysanthemums by Claude Monet is in the public domain because its copyright has expired. The painting is in the collection of the Metropolitan Museum of Art, New York.

45. The celestial sphere is from *Scenography of the Ptolemaic Cosmography*, by Johannes van Loon, based on Andreas Cellarius's *Harmonia Macrocosmica*, 1660. It is in the public domain because its copyright has expired.

46. The 1906 automobile calendar is by Edward Penfield, and is in the collection of the Library of Congress Prints and Photographs Division. It is in the public domain because its copyright has expired.

47. The 50-year perpetual calendar photograph is in the public domain.

48. The cartoon by John T. McCutcheon is from his 1905 collection *The Mysterious Stranger and Other Cartoons by John T. McCutcheon*. It is in the public domain because its copyright has expired.

License Description and Terms

Aside from material purely in the public domain, photographs and other material in this book are used under specific licenses permitting free use, usually with an attribution requirement. For full text and terms of these licenses, click or enter the appropriate links below. If you believe there is an error in the copyright status or attribution of any of these images, please email us.

- Creative Commons Attribution 2.0 Generic (CC-BY 2.0): http://creativecommons.org/licenses/by/2.0/deed.en
- Creative Commons Attribution-Share Alike 3.0 Generic (CC-BY-SA 3.0): http://creativecommons.org/licenses/by-sa/3.0/
- Creative Commons Attribution-Share Alike 2.5 Generic (CC-BY-SA 2.5): http://creativecommons.org/licenses/by-sa/2.5/deed.en
- Creative Commons Attribution-Share Alike 2.0 Generic (CC-BY-SA 2.0): http://creativecommons.org/licenses/by/2.0/deed.en
- Creative Commons Attribution-Share Alike 1.0 Generic (CC-BY-SA 1.0): http://creativecommons.org/licenses/by-sa/1.0/deed.en
- CC0 1.0 Universal (CC0 1.0) Public Domain Dedication (CC0 1.0) http://creativecommons.org/publicdomain/zero/1.0/deed.en
- GNU Free Documentation License (GFDL): http://en.wikipedia.org/wiki/Wikipedia:Text_of_the_GNU_Free_Documentation_License
- License Art Libre (Free Art License): http://artlibre.org

Other Books from Timespinner Press

The Story of a Special Day
Michael Dobson

A series of (eventually) 366 volumes covering everything that happened on your special day! Events, births, deaths, quotes, holidays, and much more. It's like a birthday card they'll never throw away!

US$7.95 print / US$2.99 ebook.

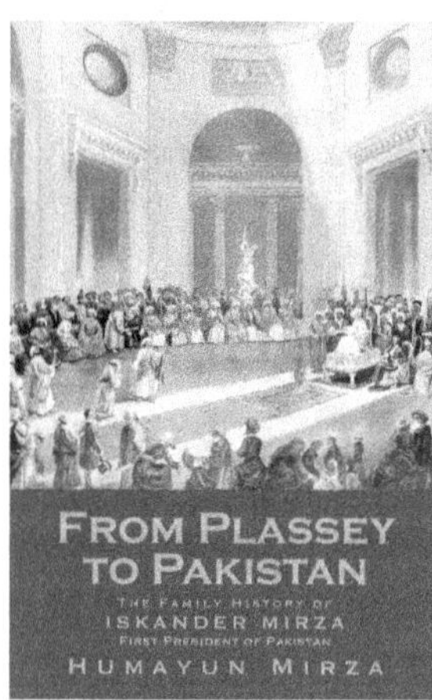

From Plassey to Pakistan
Humayun Mirza

The history of British Colonial India and the formation of Pakistan from the unique perspective of the son of Pakistan's first president and last of the royal line of Bengal, Bihar, and Orissa! This unique historical document tells the inside story of this distinguished family, including the detailed story of the coup that toppled his father from power!

US$27.95 print

A Whole New Navy: America's War in the Pacific

Miles Durr

The most comprehensive and detailed description of America's naval war in the Pacific ever—every battle, every ship, every task force and every task group from Pearl Harbor through the Japanese surrender! A must-have for the collection of every World War II buff!

US$29.95 print

Improbable History: The Weird, the Obscure, and the Strangely Important

edited by Michael Dobson

From the birth of Western civilization to the rescue of Apollo 13, from the Leaning Tower of Pisa to Florence's Duomo, history has often turned on small, improbable details. Whatever happened to the ancient Samaritan people? Why did a fortuitous rainstorm allow the British to conquer India? How did an air raid in Italy lead to the development of chemotherapy? What happened when Albert Einstein met Adolf Hitler on the streets of Berlin? How did the Japanese manage to attack the US mainland using balloons? A cast of award-winning writers tackle some of the strangest tales in history!

US$19.95 print

The Letters of William Philip Schwartz 1842-1855

edited by John F. Schwartz

The 19th century soldier and adventurer William Philip Schwartz wrote a series of vivid and detailed letters chronicling his adventures in the Indian Wars, the Mexican-American War, the Gold Rush, and his term as Marine sergeant aboard the USS Constellation. A pioneer in photography, he took *the first known war photographs*. An unforgettable first-hand look into life in the 19th century!

US$17.95 print

Timespinner
Press

www.timespinnerpress.com